Home Leave

REBECCA JUNG

Copyright © 2018 Rebecca Jung

All rights reserved.

ISBN: 1986535983
ISBN-13:9781986535984

DEDICATION

To all Expats and Third Culture Kids, wherever you are.

CONTENTS

Acknowledgments	i
On Being Transferred to the Congo	1
Steel Town Muse	2
Haute Cuisine	3
Home Leave	5
Monkey Business	11
How to Curtsy	15
Our Father's Guide to Parenting	17
Homesick	23

ACKNOWLEDGMENTS

I'd like to thank Lori Jakiela and the Trafford Writers Workshop for their support, help, and most importantly their patience. And a very special thanks to my sister, Victoria Vance, for her love, memories, and assurances that, yes, this really did happen.

ON BEING TRANSFERRED TO THE CONGO

Stamped FRAGILE,
My father cracked open the water-stained crates
like ancient caskets,
exhuming silver nut bowls
black-enameled coffee tables,
and gardening gloves still caked
with the dry, brown soil from the cornfields
of Ohio.

Now we live in the neighborhood
of mountain gorilla, the great silverbacks,
where the thick red earth pours
in bloody clots every afternoon
turned black as night,
when the rain hurls itself at
the steaming ground with
such violence that we have to
shout to hear each other,
finally, giving up.

STEEL TOWN MUSE

Where is the man
with the honey brain and wool arms
to love and embrace me?
He will have the hot
steely smell of work and the solid
meat of muscle on bone. He will
watch me with sweet Jesus doe eyes
and we will ride in my car called Logic
that runs without gas –
a rusted, perfect machine.

HAUTE CUISINE

My father wasn't a religious man; we didn't go to church and it didn't help that there weren't any Protestant churches in most of the places we lived. We were Lutheran, but in a pinch, we could settle for most of the other Protestant denominations – even the Baptists. But the Catholic church was strictly forbidden.

As Lutherans, it was drilled into us that Catholicism wasn't exactly the work of the devil, but close enough. Catholics were idolaters that, rather than follow the bible, worshipped the gaudy, showy statues in their churches. Worse than that, Catholics were sneaky. They'd try to lure Protestants into marrying them and then insist that their children be raised as Catholics.

To marry a Catholic was to fall from grace.

And what was this thing called *purgatory*? "It's not in the Bible," my mother said. End of discussion.

Nevertheless, I secretly liked the statues of the saints, of Mary, of Jesus writhing on the cross, tears coursing down his drawn face. I was fascinated by the elaborate rituals, especially when they used incense.

Why couldn't we have even a little of that?

Religious or not, however, my father was a better Lutheran minister than the best of them. He liked to preach to my sisters, Victoria and Leslie, and me. The Little Boy Who Cried Wolf was a staple, but his all-time favorite was The Little Boy Who Refused to Eat the Nice Lady's Food.

It went something like this:

A cowboy and his little son were riding across the plains out west when they came across a little house out in the middle of nowhere. A nice old lady lived there all by herself and she was so happy to see people that she welcomed the two of them in for a hot meal. The cowboy and his son accepted her hospitality and sat down at her little wooden table, where she filled their bowls with hot stew.

But just as the little boy put his spoon in his bowl, a dead rat floated to the surface. He dropped his spoon and jumped up, knocking his chair over backwards. There's a rat, he yelled, and he refused to eat the nice lady's stew. She was heartbroken.

The cowboy grabbed his son by the collar and dragged him outside where he gave him the whupping of his life. When you're a guest and food is put in front of you, the cowboy told the little boy, you eat it. And you like it.

When we were transferred to Bukavu in the Democratic Republic of Congo, my father got there two weeks before we did, and my mother, with three little girls in tow, came later. None of us had ever been on an airplane before.

It was 1958, so we flew in a cramped Pan Am prop from the Akron/Canton airport in Ohio, to New York, and across the Atlantic to Morocco, Leopoldville, and finally to the grass landing strip near Bukavu. The trip was over 8,500 miles long.

When we crossed the equator, the stewardess gave all the passengers a certificate.

My dad ran to meet us as we stumbled down the moveable ramp steps from the plane. He hugged and kissed all of us. He was so excited, he couldn't stand still or stop talking.

"It's so good to see you guys. I've missed you so much. You're going to love it here. Wait till you see the house, Bonnie. You're going to love it. It's big, bigger than our house in Canton. There's a big yard, too. You'll have your own room, Becky. Leslie and Victoria, your room looks out over the yard. You're going to love the yard, it's so big."

We, on the other hand, had transformed somewhere over the Atlantic into zombies. My dad had to pull and push us into his little VW bug.

But rather than take us to our new home, he drove us directly to a small elegant patisserie in town, where he proudly ushered us through the door. He introduced us to an older well-dressed woman behind the glass counter. Speaking French, my father explained that this was his family and we'd come all the way from America. Then we sat down at one of the white wrought-iron café tables, and my dad ordered all of us French pastries.

Back in Ohio, dessert was my grandmother's apple pie or Hostess Ding Dongs. But what was placed in front of me was a small square of yellow cake saturated in brandy, iced in a delicate mocha cream, with mocha-flavored butter piping, topped with a coffee bean.

I took a bite and promptly threw up.

My dad jumped up, grabbed me, and apologized profusely as he hustled us out of the shop. Tight-lipped, the woman began to mop the floor.

I'd been ready for monkeys, elephants, even stew with rats in it. A French pastry was the last thing I'd expected.

HOME LEAVE

After we'd lived in Istanbul, Turkey, for two years, Goodyear Tire and Rubber, the company my father worked for, flew my family back home to Canton, Ohio. It was the 1960s, and it was Goodyear's policy that employees assigned overseas return to their stateside homes every two years for a month's home leave.

"Your grandparents hardly ever get to see you girls," my mother told my sisters and me. "This is the least we can do for them."

And so, for a month, my dad and mother, my sisters, Victoria and Leslie, and I lived with my grandparents and our Aunt Mary in their one-bathroom, two-bedroom brick bungalow. We slept in the attic, which was refurbished with wood paneling and outdoor carpet.

Aunt Mary was in her thirties and had never left home. She'd been born with cerebral palsy and couldn't walk or talk.

Her head lolled around on her neck, as if it were unsupported. Her hands, which were pale and waxy, clasped and twisted each other. When she did stand up with my grandfather's help, her skinny white legs – feet clad in white socks and saddle shoes – would flop around and buckle beneath her.

All of Mary's teeth had been pulled out, so she twisted her face into a knot around her hollow mouth. The only noises she made were high-pitched wails and grunts. Every day, she sat in a chair in her bedroom that my grandmother had put together for her.

Yellow. Mary's room was decorated in yellow. She even had yellow pajamas. Yellow was Mary's color, my grandmother said.

At night, my grandmother changed Mary into her yellow pajamas and my grandfather picked her up and carried her to her bed. Then he shut off the light and closed the door.

"We took her to doctors," my grandfather said. "They all said the same thing: put her in Apple Creek State Asylum and move on. But your grandmother wouldn't do it."

"This is mine to bear," she said. "Nobody would care for Mary the way we do. Every day, all day, all night. Nobody else would do this much."

She said, "We used to take her to church, but the others didn't like it. They didn't think it was right. I could tell. They thought we should have put Mary away. I could tell they wondered what we'd done to deserve her.

"So, your grandfather goes to church and I stay home," my grandmother sighed.

Occasionally, my grandparents would take Mary out for a car ride. She sat in the back, strapped in with the safety belt, and wrung her hands. Occasionally, she'd look out the window and grunt.

"It's good for people to see what it's like to live with hardship and suffering," my grandmother said, by which she meant her own.

I hope Mary enjoyed these outings. But there was no way to tell.

In Canton, my sisters and I didn't know anyone and couldn't get our bearings in, what was for us, just another foreign country. Only this country had junk food – and a lot of it. So, while our parents caught up with friends and relatives, we caught up with Fritos, Coke, and glazed doughnuts.

And television.

The last time we watched television was when we were still wearing fuzzy pajamas with feet, sitting in the tiny living room of our own house in Canton, watching Mighty Mouse while the snow piled up outside and the windows iced up inside. To this day, the smell of Cream of Wheat with brown sugar still reminds me of black and white cartoons.

We sat in front of the television set and ate Swanson TV dinners on those tray stands. This blew Mickey Mouse and Cream of Wheat right out of the water. This was the ultimate.

Especially the Swansons Salisbury steak dinners. *A mouth-watering Salisbury steak topped with mushroom gravy alongside mashed potatoes and corn. Hope you're hungry!*

But after two weeks of TV dinners, even the Salisbury steak *and* fried chicken, none of us could stomach any more family togetherness. We'd also had our fill of my grandmother's dry, overcooked salmon patties with canned peas.

If we didn't like it, I could only imagine how Mary felt about my grandmother's cooking repertoire. Mary had her meals blended into a mush, which she was spoon fed.

"I'll bet you all haven't had a home-cooked meal in a long time," my grandfather said, looking at my mother.

"Bonnie doesn't cook. She has a maid do it for her," my grandmother said. "Isn't that right?"

My mother looked down at her plate. She didn't say anything.

They were partially right – my mother was a horrible cook, probably because she'd grown up on home-cooked meals like these, so in Turkey she left the cooking to either me or the maid.

A word about maids and chauffeurs is in order here.

Any time I mention that my family had servants and sometimes chauffeurs overseas, people's eyebrows go up and they roll their eyes. It holds no weight if I try to explain that it had nothing to do with having money – all expat families had servants.

They were the liaisons between our families and the countries we were dropped into where we not only didn't speak the language, but also knew nothing of the culture. The servants knew the best street markets to buy food and how to haggle over the prices. They taught us the customs and the basics of living in their country.

For example, in Bukavu, Democratic Republic of Congo, one of our servants, Raphael, showed us how to remove chiggers from our feet, which thereafter, we did every Sunday.

A chigger is a kind of flea that burrows into your feet, especially around the toenail, and lays its eggs. When this happens, you get an itchy, stinging sensation where the eggs are. Thanks to Raphael, we became experts at digging them out. Removing chiggers became one of the highlights of our week.

This is what you resort to when you don't have TV.

Chauffeurs knew how to negotiate the roads, most of them cobblestone or dirt, some of them formerly goat trails. There was no infrastructure, no zoning. In some countries, there were no traffic signs or stop lights. It was a map-less free-for-all. When we lived in Sao Paulo, Brazil, the expat community had a running joke: don't, whatever you do, pick your nose in the car, because if you come to a quick stop, you might give yourself a lobotomy.

So yes, in Turkey my mother left the cooking to either me or the maid.

We ate bourek, flaky pastry leaves cut into triangles filled with feta and spinach; rice pilaf with pine nuts; beef stroganoff; grilled bluefish, or lüfer; and piyaz – a white bean salad with chopped onions, peppers, dill, parsley, tomatoes, cucumbers, and lots of olive oil. One of our staples was feta cheese with ekmek – the local crusty sourdough bread.

As a treat, we'd buy simits, small sesame-encrusted circular breads, from street vendors. The simits had holes in their centers and vendors carried them on long poles

Or roasted chestnuts. Roasted chestnuts with their oily dark brown shells curled back from the slit where they'd been cut, exposing their sweet golden flesh. The vendors roasted and sold them from their trolleys. Now, whenever I smell that rich aroma, I'm back in Taksim Square.

I offered to make bourek one evening, but my grandfather cut me off in mid-sentence.

He said "I don't want any weird or fancy food. The meals your grandmother makes are good enough for me and you, too."

But what about Mary? I thought. Wouldn't bourek mush be better than salmon patties and canned peas mush? Wouldn't anything?

My mother reminded us that both my grandparents came from Reynoldsville, a little coal-mining town in northern Pennsylvania. They moved to Ohio where my grandfather got a job as a guard at Republic Steel. My grandmother was a full-time mother and housewife. They'd never been outside of Ohio or Pennsylvania. And, to be fair, my grandmother did try to make new dishes: mixed fruit Jell-O salad, salmon casserole surprise, and broccoli with cheddar cheese. But my grandfather was a hard-core dry-salmon-patty-canned-peas kind of guy. American was the only cheese he liked.

On the third week of living with my grandparents and Mary, my grandmother suggested that we all bathe once a week because of the last water bill. This, despite the money my father gave my grandparents to cover any extra expenses we incurred.

It was the cue for us to pile into the rented Impala, peel out of the driveway, and hit the road in search of the real America. My dad decided that was the Smoky Mountains.

We traveled the backroads of Tennessee and North Carolina and stayed in motels with pink neon lights that flashed "Vacancy." Put a quarter in a metal box and the bed vibrated.

I ate BLTs with fries and drank Coke in diners with wooden statues of Indians in full headdress that stood outside the doors. I talked my father into going to The Little Brown Jug, a restaurant built like a log cabin. If we got hungry while we were on the road, we'd stop and get ring bologna and Swiss cheese to eat in the car. We canvassed the tourist gift shops and bought Stuckey's pecan logs and turtles.

My dad timed the trip so we got back to my grandparents' with just a few days to spare before we flew back to Turkey. But a few days was all my grandmother needed to get her last licks in, and in the past two years she'd built up quite a reserve of venom.

This was a side of my grandmother I'd never known about. I don't know about my sisters, but it came as a shock to me.

My grandmother was the person who wrote how much she missed us in letters that we couldn't wait to get. She wrote about all the things we'd do when we came back: Picnics in McKinley Park; trips to Cook Forest to look at the autumn leaves; Sunday after-church lunches with her homemade pies. A lemon-meringue pie made just for my sister Leslie, because it was her favorite. A warm custard pie with nutmeg sprinkled on top for me.

Lemon meringue pies were a challenge – only the tips of the meringue peaks should be browned; but custard pie was the most difficult. My grandmother was an artist when it came to pies.

One time, when it was just my grandmother and me, I sat in the kitchen and watched her roll out the crust between two sheets of waxed paper. She taught me her secrets for making the perfect pie.

She said "Don't over-bake custard pie, or the custard comes out separated from the crust and rubbery. Don't under-bake it, or it'll come out a soupy mess, the crust mushy. But when you bake it just enough, the custard has small beads of sweat on it and the crust is flaky all the way through. You'll know how long to bake it. You've got the knack. You'll know."

This was the person I dreamt of coming back to. This was my grandmother.

I didn't know this woman who wanted extra money for the water bill. Who used Mary, her daughter, as a badge of martyrdom. Who ridiculed my mother in front of us.

Maybe she didn't know us, either.

One morning, I overheard my mother and grandmother talking at the kitchen table. It was early. No one else was up. They were drinking coffee.

My mother said, "I miss you mother. Bill's always on the road and I'm so lonely. Nobody speaks English. The other women snub me. To them, I'm just a dumb American."

I saw my mother lean forward and touch my grandmother's arm. She said, "I love you, mother."

My grandmother picked up her cup, took a sip, and put it back on its saucer. My mother pulled her hand back.

"You think this has been easy on your father and me? You, Bill, and the girls are over there in different countries and we're back here alone. The girls don't even know their own home. You have maids to do your work. Who are you to complain?

"While here I am, doing all the housework *and* taking care of Mary, no thanks to you. No thanks to anyone. Your father and I never seem to get a break.

"When you do get back, you'll be in for a surprise," she said. "You'll just be one of us."

That's a lie.

I didn't hear this conversation – my mother told me about it. But this is one way I imagined it.

Maybe my grandmother was jealous of my parents leaving and having a bigger life than hers. Maybe she was bitter because my mother wasn't around to help care for Mary. Maybe she resented the close relationship my mother had with my sisters and me.

I imagine mostly she just liked being miserable. And the power of cruelty.

MONKEY BUSINESS

It was the 1950s, and our father wouldn't buy anything made in Russia. He was very strict about this, to the point of refusing to eat Russian caviar, even if it was offered at dinner parties. That's why, when he came home from one of his business trips while we lived in the Democratic Republic of Congo, with a spider monkey on his shoulder, we named the monkey Krushchev.

My sisters and I were thrilled. Our mother was not.

"You're never around, and I'm here holding down the fort," my mother said. "And you bring home a monkey? You know, of course, who's going to get stuck taking care of him."

"Aw, c'mon hon," my father said, smiling sheepishly. "I almost got a baby chimp. He had a runny nose and looked so pathetic."

Even I knew that was pushing it.

My mother said, "Don't you dare."

But my dad was a sucker for cute animals. He spent most of his time driving on dirt roads carved out of the bush, and he could go miles before coming across a small village of thatched huts. It must have been lonely, so I can understand why he might be tempted to buy the monkeys, apes, and birds that a lot of the Congolese children captured to sell. He was disciplined, I have to hand it to him; but there was something about the little spider monkey that broke his resolve.

So, he bought him.

I'm sure that our Belgian neighbor, Madame Obusier, chalked it up as just another idiotic venture of the stupid Americans who lived next door.

She hated us. But to be fair, she hated all Americans, as did most of the other Belgians in the Congo. They had a lot of complaints, but what topped the list was that Americans spoiled the "help."

Whereas the Belgians called the Congolese *singes* (monkeys) to their faces, we called them by their first names. At my mother's request, Sebastien and Raphael, the two man-servants we employed, brought their wives, Feza and Adimu, and their children to our house. While Sebastien and Raphael worked, my mother would sit with the women on the flagstone stoop outside the kitchen and talk about being mothers. Motherhood, regardless the cultural differences, is a universal language.

Given the way they treated the Congolese, we didn't like the Belgians, either.

Sebastien and Raphael were friends. They were Hutus from the same tribe, but they couldn't have been more different. Sebastien was serious, dignified, the consummate professional. His job as head man-servant was his vocation. He ran the household. If he had been in England, he would have been a butler to the aristocracy.

Raphael, on the other hand, would have been a court jester. He sang, he joked, and he played with my sisters and me. He also teased Sebastien unmercifully.

"He's always so serious, isn't he?" Raphael would say, mimicking Sebastien's unsmiling, serious face.

He would pick us up to tweak Sebastien's goatee. "Let's see if we can make him laugh."

Sebastien was not amused. He'd give Raphael withering looks but endured the good-natured ribbing.

Krushchev wasn't a very good pet. He didn't fetch, he didn't play with my sisters and me, and he wasn't affectionate. All he did was groom; so, he and I spent hours grooming each other, picking off imaginary fleas and ticks, which can become boring for a kid. And, being a kid, I'm ashamed to say that I eventually lost interest in him. So, poor Krushchev was left to his own devices on the second-floor balcony of our house. And, being a monkey taken from the jungle, his key device was to escape. Which he eventually did, while my father was on another one of his business trips.

We were amazed at how fast a monkey could move, especially a monkey bent on escaping. My mother, sisters, and I watched in awe as Krushchev practically flew from the balcony to a tree, then another tree, then onto the kitchen roof, and finally Madame Obusier's clothesline where her starched white sheets were hung out to dry. Unfortunately for Madame Obusier, and us, Krushchev had snagged his long tail on something during his great escape, and it was bleeding, all over the pristine white sheets.

The screams of rage from next door broke our trancelike state. We didn't have to know French to get the gist of what Madame Obusier was saying. Fury, as it turns out, is another universal language.

We ran to get Sebastien who, as the most level-headed and unflappable of all of us, immediately took charge of the situation. He grabbed a banana, climbed the wall between Madame Obusier's house and ours, and held it up to Krushchev.

As soon as Krushchev took the bait, Sebastien grabbed and scruffed him and my mom fired up her old, moldy, mushroom-infested VW bug. My sisters and I quickly squeezed into the backseat and Sebastien, still gripping Krushchev, jumped in the front. My mom stripped the gears shifting into first, and we made a beeline for the nearest jungle opening, where we came to a screeching halt. Sebastien jumped out and flung Krushchev into the bush.

Krushchev did what any sane, healthy spider monkey would – swinging from vines to branches, he got as far away from human civilization as he could.

As it turned out, he was the smart one.

Two weeks later, Madame Obusier was found dead; she'd been macheted to death.

The Congolese had finally had enough. They wanted their independence, which the Belgians refused to even consider, and Leopoldville, the capital of the Congo, exploded in three days of riots. Four-hundred people, African and European, were killed or wounded.

The African political parties that were forming gave the Congolese a way to channel and organize the rage that had been building. They stood up to their oppressors: they began talking back. They refused to obey the laws the Belgians had imposed on them. They quit their jobs as servants.

Now, Sebastien, ever the most level-headed, unflappable – and wisest – of all of us, told my father it was time for us to go. And, of course, he was right. It didn't matter that we weren't Belgian, we were white and that's all that mattered.

My dad gave Sebastien and Raphael each six months' pay and asked them to watch over the house and our belongings, which we'd stashed upstairs. Then we packed some clothes, a few essentials, and a gun, and we headed for Uganda and eventually Kenya. Before we piled into the car, my father shook Sebastien's hand and thanked him for everything.

"Be safe Bwana," Sebastien said. "Madame and the children must stay safe, as well."

As we pulled away, I turned around to look out the small back window of the car.

Sebastien was standing there, watching us as we drove off.

Four months later, my father risked going back to check on the house. There was no electricity, and he got there at night. He unlocked the front door and turned on his flashlight. He heard something in the living room, followed by footsteps. Someone was running towards him. He held up the flashlight. The beam of light broke the blackness in front of him. The footsteps stopped.

It was Sebastien. For four months, he'd slept on the couch in the house with a machete at his side.

I don't know if the two men embraced each other, maybe even shed a few tears. But I like to think so.

HOW TO CURTSY

You stand straight. You face the adult.
You take the adult's hand and shake it. Not too hard, not too limp.
You bend your right leg and place it behind the knee of your left leg. You touch the ground with the toe of your right foot behind your left foot. You bend both knees and dip.
You did this whenever you were introduced to adults, provided they weren't family friends.
When we were back in Canton, Ohio, on home leave, my dad insisted we still shake hands and curtsy. To my parent's friends. To our relatives whom we'd never met before. To Pastor Ruth and the members of the Zion Lutheran Church where my father would give short presentations with slides of the family in Africa. He did this during every home leave. And during every home leave, we curtsied.

"It shows that you're polite, that you have class," my dad told us.

"It shows that we can act like trained monkeys on display," my sister Leslie muttered under her breath.

OUR FATHER'S GUIDE TO PARENTING

The effect of independence on the Belgian civilians was dramatic. A rush of refugees came through ... official reports state that there were 3,280. One family arrived with a young child with only one shoe; they had left in such a panic that they did not look for the other.
"Towards Independence in Africa," Patrick Walker

When you're a child, you don't appreciate how dire some situations are. And then you grow up, and you think everything's dire. Forgetting to get cereal at the grocery store. Getting a parking ticket. Running late for yoga class.

Then you remember another time, another place, and just like that, your priorities shift. For me, that time, that place, is Africa

It was 1961, I was 10, and my family and I were living in Elizabethville, a lovely city in Katanga, just in time for Moise Tshombe's, the President of Katanga, battle to separate the province of Katanga from the Democratic Republic of Congo.

In 1961, Patrice Lumumba, the Prime Minister of the independent DRC, was tortured and murdered in Katanga. That same year, the UN Secretary Dag Hammarskjold was killed when his plane was shot down. He'd been on his way to negotiate peace talks between the Congolese government and Tshombe.

After that, UN troops moved into Katanga, while mercenaries on Tshombe's payroll poured in.

1961 was not a good year to be in the lovely city of Elizabethville, Katanga.

The Swedish soldiers who patrolled the streets were striking. They were tall, blonde, and their blue helmets played up their blue eyes. They thought my mom was striking, too. She was a petite platinum blonde with dynamite legs and they whistled at her whenever she walked downtown with my two sisters, Victoria and Leslie, and me trailing behind her.

The Canadians, on the other hand, were polite and friendly. Every Sunday they played baseball with the Americans.

One evening in September, my mom, sisters, and I were at the Elizabethville airport to see my dad off on one of his business trips. I remember it was raining.

My mom started to cry. She asked my dad not to leave us, to stay. The situation in Elizabethville had gotten worse, and she was afraid to be alone. I'd never seen her like this and it scared me.

My dad relented. It was the first – and last – time he ever did that. We were stunned.

Then we all walked out of the airport, my dad put his suitcase in the trunk, and we drove home.

He never talked about it and neither did the rest of us. A month later, I wasn't sure if it had even happened.

But that night, at the same airport, two groups of Canadian UN peacekeepers were waiting to leave on reconnaissance missions when a patrol of Congolese soldiers rushed them. The Congolese forced the Canadians facedown onto the tarmac and then kicked them. They beat the commanding officer until he was unconscious. After about ten minutes, the Canadians were rescued by a Danish officer and Ghanain troops.

Two days later, my dad flew out of that airport for the business trip he'd missed.

And then there was Michel Haydn.

He was a friend of the family, which meant I didn't have to curtsy when we said hello. That was just fine, as far as I was concerned. I didn't like him.

And he knew it.

"Becky, you don't like me so much, eh?" he said. "That's alright. Maybe someday."

I didn't like him because he was tan, his hair was bleached blond from the sun, and he was tall, so much so that my dad had to look up to him when they were together. I also didn't like him because he liked my mom.

He was a tragic, romantic figure from another time. He would bend over my mom's hand and kiss it, rather than say "Hello." And to round out his melancholy noble persona, he had a bad case of unrequited love for her. He saw her as a lady in distress, alone, vulnerable, in need of protection in the heart of darkness, which, in fact, she was.

HOME LEAVE

Michel was the only son of a White Russian, one of the many aristocrats who had emigrated after the fall of the Tsar, some of them opting for Africa, though god knows why. I pictured Russia as a series of vast snowy steppes dotted with an occasional village with onion-shaped spires over churches. I couldn't imagine that Russia was anything like Africa. Nevertheless, Madame Haydn, with her son, moved to the Congo.

Madame Haydn was a tall, thin woman with long white hair that she wore in a French knot. She had been a lady in the Tsar's court, and she maintained that formality.

But she was kind, gracious, and best of all, interesting. She told my sisters and me that the reason she wore red nail polish was to commemorate her two dogs that had died. She leaned over and held up her hands, fingernails painted a brilliant red.

"They are red for their blood," she said in a stage whisper. "So I shall never forget them."

After this dramatic display, neither would we.

Both Michel and his mother doted on each other; they were, after all, the last of their kind. As far as Madame Haydn was concerned, Michel could do no wrong. She brushed aside the fact that he was an alcoholic; she overlooked his long, unexplained absences. She even forgave him for being a mercenary in the French Foreign Legion.

About mid-September, 150 Irish UN soldiers of the "A" Company were deployed to Jadotville, a small, isolated mining town to the north of Elizabethville. Ostensibly, they'd been sent to protect the civilian population, but when they got there, they found that they weren't welcome. Nobody had bothered to tell them that the locals supported Katanga's secession.

Shortly after the Irish got to Jadotville, UN soldiers in Elizabethville made a strategic error – a big one, as in killing civilians that they thought were firing on them. Only they weren't. After that, as far as the Katangese were concerned, that meant it was open season on killing anyone with a blue helmet on. And that included "A" Company.

The only instructions the Irish had been given were that, as peacekeepers, they were not to fire their weapons; but when the they found themselves surrounded by 3,500 Katangese and mercenaries who opened fire on them, they decided to bag that command.

The Irish defended their position, but on the sixth day they had run out of ammunition, water, and food; their transportation had been destroyed by mortars; and their requests for reinforcements ignored. Their only recourse was to surrender, which they did.

Riots broke out in Elizabethville. The locals stoned UN armored vehicles and burned civilian cars. A mob of Katangese sacked the Hotel Leopold I and attacked the UN soldiers there.

I knew that hotel. We'd stayed there until my dad found us a house. I remembered that the hotel had a large, brightly lit dining room, and the service was good. So was the food, especially the steak au poivre and dame blanche.

But now it was a full-scale war, and Elizabethville was the battlefield.

The house my father had found for us was miles from the city, near the bush. There were no neighbors, no shops, no paved streets. We lived in the only house on a dirt road that got washed out every time it rained.

This was typical.

Every time we got transferred, which could be anytime, but invariably during the school year, my father would come home and announce the next place we'd be living. It happened so often, we recognized all the signals. We knew the drill. My father was, if nothing else, consistent.

He was always so excited, so confident that he'd convince us that *this* time it would be different.

"You kids are lucky. Anybody else would give their eye teeth to see the things you do. The advantages you have," he'd say.

He was so transparent.

Bukavu, DRC – "Elephants! Lions! Giraffes! Think of the advantages."

Elizabethville, Katanga – "Elephants! Lions! Giraffes! And we'll be living in a European city with stores, tree-lined boulevards, and people who speak English! Think of the advantages."

Istanbul, Turkey – "Mosques! Minarets! Belly dancers! It's called the Dirty Pearl of the East! Think of the advantages."

All I could think of was, what about Paris, France? London, England? How about Milan, Italy? There must be plenty of advantages to living in those places.

"He missed his calling," my sister Leslie said. "He should have been a travel agent."

The rest of the routine was also predictable.

My dad would move to the new place before the rest of us, leaving my mom to oversee the move while he got the lay of the land and found us a house.

Our possessions were usually shipped by boat, so everything was packed into big wooden crates that were built around them. Months later, when they were finally delivered to our new home, it was like Christmas. My dad would get out the crowbar and tear the crates down. I remember the sound of creaking and splintering wood, the sound of slats hitting the floor, and the smell of wet wood.

Most of the time, our furniture and clothes were water stained. I imagined our crates in the cargo hold of a ship that was being tossed around like a cork in the ocean, waves crashing over the hull, sailors running around in a panic, the captain strapped to the steering wheel.

While our crates got soaked.

When we finally did arrive in the new place, my dad would meet us at the airport. While we went through customs and squeezed our suitcases into the car, he would extol the virtues of our new home. It would go something like this:

"Hon, you're going to love it. There's a big master bedroom, and girls, listen to this, each of you will have your own room. There's a big living room and the dining room is pretty big, too. There are a lot of windows. And closets, lots of closets. There's only one bathroom, but hon, wait until you see it – it's big, and the toilet works."

"What about the kitchen?" my mom would ask.

"The kitchen," my dad would say, as if he'd forgotten it. "The kitchen is a little small, but it's got a newer refrigerator. The stove's a little older and not real big, but there are windows in the kitchen that look out over the yard. There's enough room for you to plant a garden, Becky. Imagine."

Having been uprooted again and cooped up in a plane for god knows how long, my mother, sisters, and I were drained and in zombie mode, which was a good thing.

The places my dad found were always miles from civilization, such as it was. Sometimes the house would have a wall around it.

"It's to keep us in and everyone else out," my dad would say.

So, while he was somewhere on one of his many business trips, we were alone.

One night, in Elizabethville, when my dad was out of town, someone pounded on our front door. My mom stood up. She looked at my sisters and me and then at the door.

We heard someone yelling outside. It was a man and he was speaking English.

My mom opened the door and Michel Haydn walked in. He didn't say anything. He closed the door behind him and locked and bolted it.

"Elizabethville is being bombed," he said. "Rebel mobs are roaming the streets and countryside, killing and looting." Then he stopped and looked at me and my sisters. "It's late, yes? Shouldn't the girls be in bed?"

"Yes," my mom said. "C'mon girls, to bed." She walked us into our bedroom, shut off the light, and closed the door.

I could hear the two of them talking in the living room, but couldn't make out what they were saying. Then I fell sleep.

Michel slept on our couch that night with a gun under his pillow. The next morning, he was gone. I don't remember ever seeing him again.

One time, I asked my dad what he thought of Michel and our mom being together so much while he was away.

He looked surprised.

He said, "Michel was just checking in on you guys, and I'm glad he did. I couldn't, you know that. I was on the road a lot, so I could support you guys. And I got the Litchfield International Award of Merit because I did such a good job. Remember that? Remember I flew back to the States to go to the ceremony while we were living in Nigeria?"

He was sitting at the dining room table, his work papers spread out. He stopped and stared at the papers.

"It's not like I wanted to be away all the time," he said.

"As for your mother, she doesn't even look at other men. She'd never cheat on me. I've never had to worry about that. She's not that kind of woman."

Years later, after we'd left Africa and were living in Istanbul, Turkey, my sister Victoria told me about a weekend when the family made a trip to Ephesus. It was the birthplace of the Virgin Mary, the mother of Jesus.

I'd heard what Jewish mothers could be like and I wondered if Mary had been like that, too. Always worried. Interfering. Overprotective. It would have been hard with a son like Jesus. Even for a Catholic mother.

The grounds at Ephesus were pockmarked with large black holes that had been deep wells. The stone walls that had encircled them had crumbled to dust over the centuries, so there was nothing to keep anyone from falling in.

My dad was walking with Victoria by his side. They were picking their way around the wells and rubble.

My dad said, "I wish I hadn't brought you girls here."

Victoria looked up at him, but he wasn't talking to her. He was looking at the holes, not her.

"It's dangerous," he said. "You could fall in."

HOMESICK

The first time I got homesick, I was 8 years old and living in the Democratic Republic of Congo.

My father worked for Goodyear Tire and Rubber Company in the Export Division, and this overseas assignment was the first of many. It was 1958, and my parents, my sisters – Victoria and Leslie – and I had been transferred to Bukavu, a city in the Democratic Republic of Congo.

One Friday night, I overheard my father tell my mother that he could really go for a pizza right now. They both laughed. "You call Zavarelli's and I'll go pick it up," he said. They laughed again. And then it hit me as if an electric shock had jolted me: I couldn't get pizza. I might never be able to get pizza again.

The sudden sense of loss was so incomprehensible, intolerable, that there was no way to express it. It went deeper than speaking, than crying. I was a little girl with no moorings, no anchor, no roots, in free fall. My stomach dropped, and I became nauseous.

I love to travel, but to this day, when I leave a country, when I wheel my luggage to the gate, when I get ready to board a plane, I get sick to my stomach. I have to fight the urge to go to the bathroom and vomit.

It has nothing to do with being airsick. It has everything to do with leaving. Again.

And I'm not the only one who endures this. Others who grew up as expats also experience it. Davut, a friend of mine from Turkey, goes through the same thing. His father had been a Turkish diplomat, and the family was constantly on the move. "It takes all the discipline I have to enter a plane," he told me. "Once we're in the air, I'm fine; but until then, it's almost unbearable."

Wherever we were living, the highlight of our day was when the mail came. If there was a pale blue onion-skin envelope with Par Avion written on it, it was a letter from my grandmother. The envelope, which weighed almost nothing, opened into a letter, which was crammed full of my grandmother's tiny cursive.

She wrote about what was happening back in America – in Canton, Ohio – our home. The latest television shows, like Soupy Sales and Laugh In. What our relatives, whom my sisters and I barely knew, were up to.

"There are huge stores now," she wrote. "K-Mart, Topps Carousel, and Giant Tiger, where you can buy anything."

To be able to go into a store and buy children's clothes was beyond our imagination. All my sister's and my clothes were made at home. My mother was a good seamstress, but every once in a while she'd look at us and shake her head. "You girls look like you just got off the boat," she'd say. "You look like missionary kids."

Ten years and 10 countries later, I was shipped back to Ohio to go to college.

Now, I'd be able to talk to my grandmother and not wait a week or more to continue a conversation. I'd walk into one of those huge stores and buy ski pants, or whatever else was in style. I'd watch television, which I hadn't seen since I was 7.

I'd go to supermarkets, which my grandmother said were also bigger. I hadn't been in a supermarket in 10 years.

So, this time, when my plane lifted off from Heathrow, bound for Canton, Ohio, I wasn't sick; I was elated. It was surreal. I was going home, and not just for home leave. I was going back home for good.

Before I left, my parents gave me a list of things to do:

Go to Heggy's, on West Tusc, sit in one of the high-back wooden booths, and order a cheeseburger with the works, French fries with a pat of butter on them, and a chocolate milkshake so thick the straw stands up. And think of us.

Go to Harry London's Chocolate and get a bag of their homemade filled chocolates. The raspberry creams, no, the coconut creams are the best. Think of us.

Order a pizza from Zavarelli's with everything but anchovies and eat it while you watch the late-night movie on TV.

But, when I asked where Heggy's was, nobody knew. You want a real cheeseburger? Go to Burger King or McDonald's. McDonald's has the best fries.

I did go to London's, but instead of a small shop where the owners waited on you, it was a spacious, brightly lit store that sold ready-made chocolates and small gifts. Harry wasn't there anymore; he'd sold out to Fannie May, a national chain. Nevertheless, I did buy a few cream-filled chocolates. They were okay, but we'd grown up on Godiva chocolates when we'd lived in Brussels. Those confections were so delicate we had to rush home before they melted. They were made with fresh cream and no wax.

And the pizza? I ended up throwing it in the garbage. It didn't come close to the small pizzas in Florence, which were way better than the pizzas in Naples.

When I did go to one of the many supermarkets, I got as far as the breakfast food aisle where I stood, bewildered by all the different cereals there were. I walked out empty handed.

Too late, I realized that I'd pinned all my dreams of home on my parent's memories. I'd been betrayed, but it was nobody's fault. There was no-one to blame. All I knew was that I didn't belong here, and I couldn't go back. And even if I could, where would I go? Which place? We'd been uprooted so many times, I had no base. I was a refugee from limbo, with no promised land.

.

ABOUT THE AUTHOR

Rebecca Jung's poetry and prose have been published in *MiPo, Pennsylvania Review, Pittsburgh Quarterly, The Burningword, Wazee Journal,* and *The Impetus,* as well as the *Pittsburgh Post-Gazette* newspaper. Her poetry has also appeared in two books: *Along These Rivers: Poetry and Photography from Pittsburgh;* and *Burningword Ninety-Nine, A Selected Anthology of Poetry, 2001-2011.*

In a span of 10 years, Rebecca and her family lived in 10 different countries, including the U.S., on five different continents. The first place was Bukavu, Democratic Republic of Congo. Just in time for the War for Independence.

After 10 years, she came back to the U.S. and attended Kent State. Just in time for the shootings.

She now lives in Pittsburgh, Pennsylvania, where she shares an old Victorian house with four rescue rabbits and one guinea pig.

She has no plans on moving again.

Made in United States
Orlando, FL
21 June 2024